Ballet

Susan Meredith

Designed by Nickey Butler

Additional design by Catherine-Anne MacKinnon

Illustrated by Shelagh McNicholas

Ballet consultant: Nicola Katrak

Reading consultant: Alison Kelly,
Roehampton University

Contents

What is ballet?

Ballet is a kind of dancing.

Ballet dancers make beautiful shapes and patterns with their bodies.

Ballet dancers

Dancers make ballet look easy, although it is difficult. It is hard work to do it well.

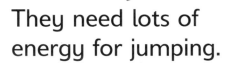

Dancers have to be strong to balance.

They need lots of energy for jumping.

They have to bend into unusual shapes.

And they must train almost every day.

Top female stars are called ballerinas.

There are usually two main stars in a ballet - a ballerina and her male partner.

It takes years of practice to do steps like this one.

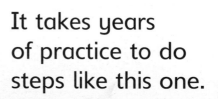

Telling a story

No one speaks in a ballet but the dancers often tell a story by the way they move.

The music helps to tell the story too.

When this good fairy dances in *The Sleeping Beauty*, the music is soft and tuneful.

The music is harsh
and scary when this
wicked fairy dances.

The dancers use signs,
called mime, in stories.

This means   This means
"I'm afraid". "Please".

Ballet steps

Ballet dancers learn lots of different steps and positions.

This position is called an arabesque.

Female dancers balance on the very tips of their toes.

One of the first ballet dancers was a French king and ballet steps all have French names.

Ballet dancers make big jumps look light and graceful. Some can do the splits in the air.

Follow the pictures to see how this step is done. It is called a pas de chat (step of a cat).

Making a ballet

For a new ballet, someone decides what steps to put with some music. This person is called a choreographer.

The choreographer works out the steps with the dancers.

The dancers rehearse their steps over and over again for weeks.

A group of dancers like this one has to move together well.

Then, they rehearse on the stage, wearing their costumes.

Ballet steps are written down in squiggles, like music.

Costumes

There are lots of different kinds of costumes in ballets.

Most of this dancer's body has been painted so he looks like a statue.

It can take hours before each show for body paint to be put on.

Dancers get used to wearing difficult costumes in rehearsals.

This rat costume is hot and heavy to dance in.

Women and men all put on make-up.

It has to be thick so their faces show up from the stage.

Tutus

A tutu is a ballet skirt made out of net. Some tutus have as many as 16 layers.

A tutu is made all in one piece. The dancer has to step into it.

Someone helps her to do it up. Tutus are made to fit tightly.

Long skirts make the dancers look soft and floaty.

In a short tutu,
a dancer can move
her legs freely.

You can see more
clearly what she
is doing.

The layers of
net make the
skirt stick out.

Dancers store their
tutus hanging upside
down so the outsides
don't get spoiled.

15

Ballet shoes

Female dancers wear special shoes when they dance on their toes.

The shoes are called pointe shoes.

Dancing on pointe makes a dancer's legs look longer.

A ballerina can wear out a new pair of pointe shoes in just one show.

Pointe shoes are stiff
and flat at the end to
help the dancer balance.

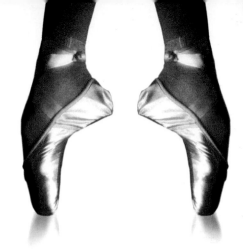

Dancers sew ribbons
inside their pointe shoes
so they can tie them on.

The shoes can hurt so
some dancers put pads
inside to protect their toes.

At first, girls learn to
balance on pointe holding
onto a rail called a barre.

Dancing in pairs

Female and male dancers often do a dance in a pair. This is called a pas de deux.

The man helps the woman to balance in tricky positions.

The man lifts the woman up.

Then he lowers her into another position.

The woman has to trust the man not to drop her.

He makes it look easy to lift her high up in the air.

Male dancers do exercises and lift weights to make themselves strong.

A dancer's life

All ballet dancers, even the top stars, do a class with a teacher almost every morning.

The class starts with lots of warm-up exercises at the barre.

Then, the dancers do slow, smooth steps away from the barre.

The class ends with fast turns, big jumps and pointe work.

After the class, the dancers rehearse. They may do a show in the evening too.

This dancer is listening to the music for her steps. She rehearses in a tutu skirt to get used to it sticking out.

Sometimes ballet dancers have to be treated for injuries.

Before the show

Lots of dancers often have to share one small dressing room to get ready for a show.

This dancer is keeping her legs warm while another one helps her get dressed.

Before the show starts, dancers do warm-up exercises.

At the right time, a loudspeaker calls them to the stage.

Dancers dip their pointe shoes in a powder called rosin so they don't slip on the stage.

These dancers are waiting at the side of the stage for their turn to go on.

The dancer on the floor has a sore leg.

23

Learning ballet

You start learning ballet by moving to music and perhaps acting out stories.

The ballet teacher shows you what to do.

You turn out your legs and feet from your hips.

Turning out helps you lift your legs higher in the air.

You point your toes to make your legs look long. You point them even when you are jumping in the air.

Some teachers put on shows. These girls are meant to be caterpillars.

Five positions

When you first start ballet, you learn two main positions to stand in.

First position   Second position

After you have been doing ballet for a while, you learn three harder positions.

Third position   Fourth position   Fifth position

Even very difficult steps usually start and finish with the dancer's feet in fifth position.

You can put arm and foot positions together in different ways.

This dancer has her feet in fifth position and her arms in fourth position.

Ballet school

If a girl or boy is really good at ballet, they might go to a full-time ballet school.

To get into the school, they have to do a test for the teachers.

They have to have exactly the right kind of body for ballet.

At the school, they do normal lessons as well as lots of dancing.

These ballet school girls
are stretching their legs
at the barre.

Ballet school children usually
live at their school except
during the holidays.

Glossary of ballet words

Here are some of the words in this book you might not know. This page tells you what they mean.

 ballerina - a female dancer who dances the main parts in ballets.

 mime - to act out in movements only, without using words.

 arabesque - a position where one leg is straight in the air behind the dancer.

 rehearse - to prepare for a show by doing the steps over and over again.

 on pointe - on the very tips of the toes. Female dancers dance on pointe.

 barre - a rail that dancers hold onto in a class to help them balance.

 pas de deux - a dance for two. Men and women do pas de deux together.

Websites to visit

If you have a computer, you can find out more about ballet on the Internet. On the Usborne Quicklinks Website there are links to four fun websites.

Website 1 - Look at lots of ballet photos.

Website 2 - Listen to some music from *The Nutcracker* ballet.

Website 3 - Print out pictures of ballet dancers to shade in.

Website 4 - Watch ballet dancers doing steps.

To visit these websites, go to **www.usborne-quicklinks.com** Read the Internet safety guidelines, and then type the keywords "beginners ballet".

The websites are regularly reviewed and the links in Usborne Quicklinks are updated. However, Usborne Publishing is not responsible, and does not accept liability, for the content or availability of any website other than its own. We recommend that children are supervised while on the Internet.

Index

Acknowledgements

Photographic manipulation: John Russell.

Photo credits
The publishers are grateful to the following for permission to reproduce material:
© **Angela Taylor** 5, 16; © **Arena PAL** (Nigel Norrington) 8; © **Bill Cooper** 1, 6, 10-11, 12, 13,
19; © **CORBIS** (Kurt Stier) 17, (Paul A. Souders) 21, (Annie Griffiths Belt) 22, (David Turnley) 23,
(Dennis Degnan) 31; © **Dee Conway** 25; © **Eric Richmond** 15; © **Getty Images**
(Frank Siteman) 24; © **Linda Rich/Dance Picture Library** 3, 7, 9, 14, 18;
© **Photos To Go** (Jeff Greenberg) 29. Photograph on page 27 by Bill Cooper.
Front cover: Gillian Revie dancing in the Royal Ballet's "Les Rendezvous". Photo by Bill Cooper.
Special Thanks to Gillian Revie and the Royal Ballet.